Suit of Lights

For the three lights:

Francesca, Brychan, Cristyn

Damian Walford Davies

Suit of Lights

seren

Seren is the book imprint of
Poetry Wales Press Ltd.
57 Nolton Street, Bridgend, Wales, CF31 3AE
01656 663018
www.seren-books.com

ISBN: 978-1-85411-493-8

A CIP record for this title is available from the British Library.

The publisher acknowledges the financial assistance of the Welsh Books Council.

Cover image: detail from 'Green George' by Clive Hicks-Jenkins
www.hicks-jenkins.com

Printed in Bembo by Bell & Bain Ltd., Glasgow.

Contents

Bee

for Francesca

Bumble or honey? I couldn't tell, not be-
ing an apiarist, which you told me

is what those widebrimmed fumigators
in English gardens call themselves, who

know their buckfast from their bombus.
It just kept thudding against the glass

and hiving off, then bombing in again
as if it knew this was the room for four-

star wintersleep. What I felt was we-
ight: a fraction of an ounce? some ounces?

– it sounded more like pounds. When I
found it humbled, downed, its body

pulsing on the gravel, I thought I should
have opened up and let her in, if only

for her trying ten, twelve, times without
my thinking once (for once) of stings.

Bird

Late heat
        like heresy;
light coming in
        refracted from
a tankered sea;
        the one farm
and dairy-cool
        church as ever;
and the strangeness
        of the sparrow-
corpse weightless
        on the nave's
glazed tiles – sidelong,
        eyes wide, wire-
claws perfectly re-
        tracted, clenched
around some little
        pain, the disgrace-
ful last evacuation
        and the relict
silence of its flitting
        witless against
chantry window and
        leper's squint,
the way out trans-
        parent into hot
and heterodox light.

Plague

Piccadilly Line.

Under the grand depart-
ment stores, Yerkes' moles
cut through Thanet sand,

clay terraces and chalky tiers
lit by shells and mica. Then
they hit the bones – a seam

of femurs, skulls and gem-
like metatarsals fell around
the cutting gear, the new

century's cocksure thorough-
fares balked by Restoration
plague pits. Catching it at Knight-

sbridge, you feel the swerve
they made, all the red-ball
bubo handgrips jerking left.

Pineapples

Castle Hall, Milford Haven, 1805.

Ezra's father's cousin's friend
was gardener there, and saw

it all go up in glass one hot
July. Mr Rotch, said Ezra, over–

saw the glazing in his whaling
gear, aimed his Thule harpoon

and cursed with what my mother
calls Nantucket vim. Ezra said

that when the panes were set,
his father's cousin's friend was

taken in and shown the ropes.
Things would grow, said Ezra.

What things? said Willy, thinking
whales and glass. Ezra said

the heads of desert island cannibals
his father's cousin's friend

was made to plant in china pots.
Wasn't it, said Ezra, the Black

Hole governor who'd sold to Mr
Rotch? Sam, who'd been to school,

said that was East, not West, but
Ezra had us hooked. That night

we scaled the walls, tacked through
mackerel light onto the lawn

and out again into the dark
towards the trophy-house.

Told you so, said Ezra. Behind
great squares of glass in candle-

bloom, a hundred burning heads
on Mr Rotch's green harpoons.

Heraldic

When the stag stepped
out of some rich man's
dark, I was pushing

seventy. The scene coll-
apsed to symbols, shields:
the stag statant argent

and at gaze against
the chase, my lights
a chevron rayonnant

on sable, leafshadows
bendypaly on mount
vert – brake, *fuck*,

brake – the deadpan
dexter hart and I
affrontant, confronté,

so close I saw it draw
breath, salient back
into some rich man's dark.

Iconoclast

for Jem Poster

William Dowsing's journal, 1644.

At Stradbrook in April, angels
in glass. I broke their wings.

At Trembly, ten cherubim and
thirty texts. And superstitious

pictures, which I took down.
Miserere me, Domine, in brass.

At Clare, one of God the Father,
and two of doves, so high I had

to climb a scaffold with the brush
and wash. At Wixo, we broke a saint

and dug the steps down to the dirt.
At Beccles, rails; and Jehovah

hiding in a niche. Seven friars
at Sudbury St James, clinching

a nun. *My Meat is Flesh indeed,*
and *My Blood is Drink,* indeed.

At Snape, eleven popish pictures
and the crown of thorns, and

sponge and nails, which I pulled
off. A trinity, and a triple crown.

At Bramfield, a pelican pecking
its breast, all gilt, and diverse Virgins

with St Peter's keys. At Linstead
Parva, sun and moon in the east

window, by the King's arms,
which I broke. At Eye, I was

the only one spied Jesus
in stone above the door.

Architect

Clapton Crabbe Rolfe, sir,
at your. – Twenty-one and

needlessly eccentric. This
temple's for my father,

who, sir, one might say,
has many mansions. French

Gothic in the main, but
the rendering's my dandy

own – particoloured con-
ical erections, trefoiled space

where lesser men would stick
sham apertures (sir, stop me

if I) red stone shafts with
stiffleaf capitals, my pul-

pit vast, with tester. See my
sandstone piers and strange

stop-chamfers? I do so take
things by the horns. High

windows make the chancel
dark? What's done there's just

as. Notice the font, though –
my one small nod to innocence.

Nightharvester

The Quantock hummocks play silly
buggers with the Cardiff lights:

on-off, on-off, until the road
plateaus three miles out of Watchet

and I drove into halogen bloody day.
The combine was a moving city-

block, the alien corn metallic.
It was theatre – like a Monster

Truck show in some mid-west super
mare. The reel consumed a ten-

foot swathe and beat the living
crap out of the crop inside;

the frowsty chaff-dust hung like
mist above three fields. This is how

the world will end – four combines
and a brutal aftermath of bales.

Ideal City

Letters to Etienne de Barras (1763–1816), architect.

1.
Sir,

I write from less than
ideal times to you in less than
ideal times about your plans
for the ideal city. Let me

introduce myself. Like you,
I look for the right place to break
a plane and make my lines
a habitable space. Less than
flush, these columns are
my elevation and cross-
section.

2.
I bought six bound sheets.
Fine; atlas-quarto with pull-
outs; calf; slight rubbing to the
spine; brown ink and pink
wash on squared-off paper.
Very rare. You know the sellers'
speak. He didn't know if there
were more than six; were there
ideal suburbs, too?

3.
I understand July 14
put paid to these plans.
Here's your city, un–

furled under my light,
its two-tone vibrant,
its levelling lines amaz–

ing. These squares could
never breed unrest –
your streets wide and

shared, conduits fanning
out to cool, factories with
fronts like grand houses.

I think nothing would ever be broken here.

4.
Your concaves: each unfilled niche
in the loggias, each un-
fussy arch
and
the bow
of the *campo*-space are
lungs and I can hear this city breathe.

5.
In this dream I was walking through fouled
streets chainstores abutting templar churches
down cul-de-sacs Blake's blessed twenty-
minute walk from South Molton Street
out *unbelievably* into *fields* bringing me up
short then ordinary unhurried men in suits
of light walking in and out of the ideal city.

6.
What would you have called
it, if they'd let you build? Time
ridicules promised cities
with drabness, conurbation,
violence, the vernacular – see
Radiant City, Garden City,
New Harmony, Urbs.

7.
Let me talk free-
ly. I admire your brothel,
shockingly municipal, laid
out in that erection only
you and I can see,
shades of pink
adding to the mis-
chief.

The Fight

Geoff Charles photograph, Tommy Farr vs Robert Eugene.

In the Kodak flash your flesh
is silver, the same age as mine.
You're still boxing clever in that

familiar crouch – head down,
reading the blows your
shadows come to. The half-

light of Rhondda booths
made six-round swells of you:
Evan Lane, Young Snowball,

Herbie Hill, coming out
fighting from the shaft. At
Harringay and Yankee Stadium

a different kind of light –
flaring, cruel, the bulbs like
shocking stars. So 1951 and you

need the purse, the 50,000
dollars of the Louis fight gone
tonypandy. *Eugene misses*

a jab and Farr pulls his. Is that a
scar you're going for? Those
ringside fellas look like brothers.

The Aria

A soldier of the invading army sings to the dying composer.

Most start to hear a music
in the shells, a rhythm to *Fire!*

Reload! Fire! We pincered
east, dodged steelballs coming

in fortissimo. The air before
a strike tunes up, and time

is caught in strange rubato.
Then you see a face blown

off, the lower jaw still rattling
yes to orders. It stands there

like a tuning fork. They sent me
in to sing. He was lying

at the centre of the city,
on a couch between two

lamps, obese as breves. I sang
the tenor aria he was famous

for, in C, some suburb-firing
as faint timpani. His eyes

conducted me. I'd never nailed
the notes so well. I stood in combat-

camouflage, held the final testing
note to no distinct applause.

Strumble Head

Pembrokeshire, scene of the French invasion, 1797.

They camped in the nave
and chantry, Exodus and
the second book of Kings

        as kindling, pissed in a switch-
        back Strumble wind against
        Ann Owen, beloved wife, et

cetera. It was amateur night.
Wales dawned on them – most
still pissed, the others hung-

        over to the tune of thirty wreck-
        ers' kegs and ten stabs at the
        Marseillaise. They strumbled

into a land of cairns and stand-
ing stones with idiot orders to
annoy. Four slurred into Brest-

        garn, its whitewash proof against
        outlandish weather; one fired a
        piece of France into a grand-

father clock that banged
Welsh time into his hammered
whiskeyhead. They slewed into

        the democratic yard, a ricochet
        of *merde!* It was all downhill
        from there to Goodwick Sands.

Chopping Board

Bought in the troubled quarter
of an hour before shops
close. On the Via di Castello

opposite the locked church
it seemed the perfect relic of
our stay – olive-wood, bevelled

edges, branded *San Gimignano*
on the bottom right of its broad
L. You knew it was absurd dis-

placement, stand-in for a space
I didn't dare ask anyone
to let me see. In kitsch ceramic

company it seemed a piece of some
true wood, something that would
seep at each bite of the knife into

the life of what we'd always be
preparing. Now its strafes and
stripes are as familiar as our

skin, its smell a censer of garlic,
lemon, pepper, cloves and game,
bloodied sometimes but sweetly

washed and rubbed with oil
and left as lovingly to dry as a
darkening fresco in the mind's eye.

Kilvert

1.
The baby was baptised in ice which was broken and swimming about in the font.

There was awkward-
ness, but he broke the ice-
crust delicately as a
brûlée;
        these, he said, the sweet
shards and bergs
that save our souls.

2.
At Rhos Goch Lane House no one was at home so I stuck an ivy leaf into the latch hole.

Improvised, so
you'd know I'd been:
a dying trefoil calling-
card, my meaning
veined on green
vellum pushed
into interior space.

When you come
in, press it between your
pages so it stains.

3.
Her pretty portrait still on the dining room mantelpiece...
On the bookshelves stood two cases of stuffed birds...

He thought they'd please
her. She thought it
cruel, that embarrassment
of birds, that parliament
of fowls between Hansard
and Hazlitt, posed
passerine, wired for flight.

  So early dead,
she said that one close
day she heard them cry for
air in the evacuated cases.

4.
It was the first time I had seen clergyman's daughters helping
to castrate lambs... they carried it off uncommonly well.

They held them like cellos,
the kneeling hands
bent to their relieving
work. It was
wrong all round. Still,

they played beautifully,
drawing something like
music from the bleating
between their legs.

5.
Very hot in morning Church, and an enormous bumble bee
crawled over the white cloth...

                        Tiger-
striped furzeball, louche
half-ounce of real
presence, had him bum-
bling through the

service, half wishing
it would sting
through each faint
dress.

6.
An angel satyr walks these hills.

Here between –
admiring cloud forms,
fancying the faster
parodies of shadow.

Here –
between the up-
lands' candour and the
valley's petty cleavages.

Now chaste,
now chafing at the collar.

7.
While I waited in the kitchen the low deep voice upstairs
began calling, "Murder! John Lloyd! John Lloyd! Murder!".

Mrs Watkins dies
like clockwork
every day at three;
her grim chiasmus
ringing out across
the farm, bringing

in her son from
carrying oats, fresh-
pressed linen
in his arms.

8.
The stories about the baboon of Maesllwch Castle grow more
and more extraordinary.

More lord than pet –
parvenu, debouching
from the shadows
like some mad déb
down the dog-
leg balusters.

Last week it made a bee-
line for the Captain's
tails and Lady Burrell's
furs, its coat of arms that
crass heraldic derrière.

9.

...on dark nights, the gentlemen pulled out the tails of their shirts and walked before to show the way and light the ladies.

The 'Dursley Lanterns' –
dapper will-o'-the-wisps
in lanes around great
houses; the phosphor-
escence of pressed Irish
linen moving in
England's dark.

For every Jill a jack-
o'-lantern, a suit of lights –

and beneath the starched
swagger of those tails
the luminous flesh-
light lanterns of the bodies.

10.

...the bag fox had been kept in a dark cellar so long that he was dazed and half blind when he was turned out.

It must have hurt like
the taste of metal
as it woke to serations of
light, the aperture

widening suddenly
into blindness.

It left the sack
flaccid, cooling, like
flayed skin.

11.
All the time we were in the tunnel these lighted matches
were travelling from hand to hand in the darkness.

The Box Tunnel pashed
the chatter, snuffed
the Flower-Show hats.
Against the black someone
struck a brim-
stone match. It passed
from man to woman like
a sacrament, hands
touching without meaning
to.
       Later, among the flowers,
he recalled the Clyro tales
of corpse candles moving
in the dark.

12.
…the young Bryants held him down in the furrow and
ploughed him into the ground.

He was a bad seed,
the sod, refused to lie
still as the plough-
knife skinned the clods.

But they sowed
Robert Jefferies deep
to see whether
his curly crop would
blossom
       into something better.

The quotations are from the diary of the Revd Francis Kilvert (1840–79).

Duomo

In the thin skin
of the terracotta dome,
red herring-
        bone bricks
bamboo-
zling us, you led me

up a thousand steps
to our honeymoon's
grand stage.

        In the cupola's
gallery, Brunelleschi's
cantilevers

holding the world
        above deep space,

we took a second to regard
each other.

        I saw you hang
there, embracing vertigo,

        a miracle

above the freight of air.

Green George

Painting by Clive Hicks-Jenkins.

Altar-
piece of spliced time:

the indie
damsel and dog an indi-

fferent audience
for the renegade cowboy-

fusilier with
Tommyhat and quilted

carmine horse
debouching from Oxwich

onto a Gol-
gotha meadow of camp-

anula to
spear a blue-tongued

gummy devil-
dragon and the tide lolls in.

Tyger, Tyger

The marble urn to Captain Colby,
mauled to death in Rawal Pinde,

1852, is at the fancy end of things,
where the better class of box pews

have their fires and flues against
the Teifi cold. From the fearful

symmetry of trophies cut by *Physick,*
London, you'd swear the man had led

an army from the forests of the night.
Rebel local rain claws at the lancets

from the Teifi floodfields. Light the box
pew fires, you cold Colby family ghosts.

Cats' Eyes

They slowed
us to a crawl,
the bitumen
men, laying
blind eyes
in hot sock-
ets of tar, the

blackspot o-
ver the brow
in bloom again,
bouquets in
bare wattle
alight with
nine lives.

Composite

Paintings by John Knapp-Fisher.

1. *Gill in a Pembrokeshire Lane*

The threat of foliage; the girl
caught in the painter's headlights, but
looking as if she's about to
draw.

2. *Llanwnda*

I know – I mean
from afterwards being
there – that off right there's
a church you've painted
elsewhere. Here, only a fore-
shortened midnight
village against that tradematt
absence of the dark: white
rambling house; the hayloft
converted later
by your son. And then

that man, a suggestion
of a stoop, sent out
in your strange weather
like a scapegoat, looking right
outside the frame: because
somewhere there, perhaps in
light, you've placed the church.

3. *Fisherman's Shed, Porthgain*

See, from the trees, the
prevailing wind? The road
tacks right, under a sky
you've worried over, under a tree
that wind is bent on
corrugating into winter.

4. *Tractor on a Skyline*

March, perhaps. Cold
enough for the exhaust
smoke to hover over
the caged driver, who sees,
without vantage, the wide
expanse of all the work
not done.

5. *Houses, Cardigan*

Someone on each thresh-
old, like doors: watching

what? The carnival or
funeral is beyond the shaker
frame.

Difficult in all this noise and all
this silence to make
out whether

those squares are chimney-
stacks continuing the line, or purged
sheets strung
wet across the street.

6. *The Birthday Walk*

Eliot's insistent lane. Follow
them, then, along that patch-
work camber – whether down or
up is up or
down to you.

7. *Manor Farm*

Amazing – that medley
of roofs hung
in feudal deep space.

What language will those
three, docked
in that capsule of a porch,
speak?
What will the martins,
returning to de Gower's
farm, breathe?

8. *Abereiddi Evening*

Sudden ill-
umination,

like a bomb going off, off
left, as in fifties news-
reels from Pacific tests where
soliders in shorts, like kids
at the end of their count, turn
to face the stunning after-
blast, and a very English
voice makes absolute
sense of it all.

Here, white-
blast cottages at dark,
and a street
lamp like a question-
mark, enquiring whether
anyone's left to watch.

9. *Nevern Bridge with Figures*

Frail, now, and drawn
delicately as the curve
of the bridge;
the hand that is not in his
extended to anticipate
a fall.
She should know
that where this image ends
the road begins
to climb, though her poise
suggests she'll cross that bridge
when she comes to it.

10. *Girl in a Rape Field*

Yellow violence: the scare-
crow girl fending
off the crop; tyre
tracks converging
to an accident.

Yellow violence; her patch-
work skirt a minor
landscape, her
semaphore bringing whom
in over the dark
cairns to land?

Lessons

for Gwyn Constantine, born 21 June 2006

Born into optimum
light, were you sensing the contraction
of days?

In the garden, your brother
was teaching my son how to scale
the world,

mackerel in their silver
shrouds falling off their
bones.

A Tilt

of the world gives the nod
to winter. There. Did you feel it,

barometer-heart, gauge
the few bars' fall, the down-

sizing of summer,
sense each inch of

flesh take on the new-
old hibernal pressure?

Salt Islands

1. Islander (Ronald Lockley, Skokholm)

Skokholmist, ambassador to the puffin
slums, coneyman, cocklolly-watcher,
salvager of spars, mapper of the dark
guts of burrows, counter of Mother
Carey's Chickens before they've hatched.

2. Island Ferry, Caldey

The kind of heat that brings the raw
smell-of-things out: refuse baking
in a dustbin, leafmulch of the holy
wells, thrift prodigal on coastal
paths. There were small deaths in-
land of dogs and caged birds – 'perished',
the radio said, as if they had souls.

He spent his last five days riding
the ferry through the sea-
frets of Caldey Sound, declining land-
fall, passing away between sand and sand.

3. Grassholm

Immaculate now
in its summer coat
of gannet-shit, moulting
into undistinguished
brown when the blitz-
birds scramble
south.

4. Ramsey

We inched clockwise,
struck into clefts
of rough time kept
by auks and fulmars, read
the spliced syntax of
rock, always brought up
short by seal commas
on stormbeaches and
cormorant question marks
on high stacks.

5. Skomer

Skalm, Skalmeye, Skawlmey –
Norse sea-caws
in Welsh Sound.

Groundsman

I remember him healing
divet-scars, tacking from try-
line to 22, penalty box to touch.

Summer had him reading
fractures on the cricket pitch,
seeding the bowler's lanky

line, botanising at silly-
mid-on. Mornings brought
chicken-fenced plots of

earth, small custodies of hurt.
Stationed now on other
ground, he stitches tears

on artificial turf, drives hover-
hoovers on tradename grass,
all-weather-man. We hail

each other; the echo amplifies
the slip from field to pitch,
groundsmanship to astro–husbandry.

Poems in Bad Weather

1. Leaves

Beyond unseasonal:
the June squall
                rips
        into the road-

side ashtrees,
sending   ser-
                ations
of sudden
            green
                    birds

into the swifts' chicane.

2. Tailback

I move: they accept
stoically
the wipers'
        smack-in-the-face.

3. Exodus

Seven cows art-
iculate bonily from a brown

spate. What language
for their after-
image except
            Nilotic, Pharaonic, lean?

4. Worksite

The nave's all snakes
and ladders. Up there,

small steel monkey-
angels with holy hods

plugging all the
holes in heaven.

High Wind

On the whitewashed corbel
I left a pebble from the pil-
grim beach – brown, a vein

of burgundy – to marinate
overnight in whatever's
distilled here when the lights

go out. I came to collect it
in a high wind, felt for it on
tiptoe. The seam had faded

to the thrift of pink, the brown
to greyish-green. What it was
flooded with I couldn't feel,

hearing only that sceptical wind
ring a tinny bell – passionately
at first, then just for the hell of it.

Aerial

for Toby Driver

1.

[SM9519]   Taking off was ceding
                                our shadow, seeing it

[SM9727]   scissor north to ruffle
                                over tilth and buckle

[SN0431]

[SN0730–0729]   at field borders, only
                                to find it waving

                                towards us up hill-
[SN1533]   fort ramparts, returning

                                through the repressed
[SN1137]   estrangement of air.

2.

Shifts / to raking light //
ground dimpling /

to tump and motte //
we bank / over the dead

giveaway of parch-
mark / ditchwork /

dyke // green tumours /
shadow brings to light.

3.
At the mountain's skirt,
        the Norman order
        of stripfields breaks

into limber lines
of Iron-
        age vernacular, tracks
                and rosaries
                of rock
pending
        on glacial
                angles. Free verse
                        above blank burgage.

4.
This map's rude as flesh
laid bare under the knife –

pathology of peninsular
ground in scar-

lets, lilacs, creams; a quarry
cirrhotic near an airfield's

sutured runway, burst
capillaries of single-track

roads, contours fanning
down from suspect nodes.

5.

Smoke from gorse fires –
the year detonates

                in seed-pods and spikes.

Burnt ground forgets itself
in air, re-

        calls itself as cloud.

Mullo

Wealthy Romans entertained themsevles at dinner parties by watching a dying mullet change colour. Seneca has an account in Natural Questions.

Nothing kills me,
       Marcus,
quite like a dying mullet,
         its frantic kissing
pulsing colour through
               scales of light.
A dead fish
       is yesterday's sorry
news. It's the dying
           does it, yes? –
this glass a window on
a body's rainbow
       throes. See the ruby
       belly blood
           turn ochre,
                brown?
       There, blue under the jaw –
now green,
       grey here,
           now pale.
       Let's not
demean ourselves by
eating it.
       See?
       It's gone out like a lamp.

Witch Scenes in time of Civil War

1. Hanging

Five are turned off in a green May. Witch one
was still when witch two's love of life described
an arc. Witch three squitched and squittered when
witch four had come to rest; witch five was neck-
and-neck but lost it at the end. Witch two kept
twitching like a snooker finger tapping baize.

2. Boy

I'm the one
shot Boy,
Prince Rupert
's mutt, at
Marston. Got
promoted for
it. God, he
snarled. I saw
him skirring
round the fancy
dressers and the
guns. All the
broadsides said
he was a witch-
dog. Came flying
in through stink-
smoke, bloody
great black thing
he was. I was
cocked when our
muzzles met.

3. Woodcut: Witches' Sabbath

Goodwife West and Mother Grayson,
girls gone bad, are dancing with

three devils. Goodwife West looks like
the Queen of Clubs; Mother Grayson's

back is turned. The devils sport deep-
cut salesman smiles. Desporting near

are cute familiars named like bottled
beers: Pye-wackett, Frisker, Barley Tom.

A decent-looking bloke plays bag-
pipes in a beech tree's fork; the scrag-

land bears a Presbyterian frown. Two
ravens hurt the sky as fleurs-de-lis.

The scenes are from Malcolm Gaskill, Witchfinders (2005).

Loft Gothic

We entered attic space
    as astronauts, moved

gingerly in novel air
    and screwball light,

looking for a brief ec-
    lipse of life downstairs.

Near a fifties leather bag
    and antique tea-chest,

a pipistrelle, picked clean
    by time and place,

lay crucified – lunar-white,
    the empty belfy

of the rib-cage loud
    with tintinabulations

of a tiny heart, the tail
    a little rosary, its span

a gangling fan of fingers,
    its blackness beating

ghostly over a micro-
    suit of lights.

The Destroying Angels

Paintings by Glyn Morgan.

1.
Bad angels in pallid
drag, flaccid puffballs
cruising over a pastoral
perhaps beautiful
enough to out-
face them.

2.
We are gorgeous
as you feared – growths
of the ground you man-
aged to heat until
we came.

3.
Amanita virosa, fungus fruit-
ing into stipe and cloud
we dare not pic-
ture.

Fair

Studt's caravanserai trails November
into town, hunkers on hardcore, caged
and concertinad. Overnight the painted

ladies – airbrushed tutelaries – undress
on metal backboards; rides unfurl like
flowers. Putting out the bins you hear

the fragments thrown from cloud banks
and surrounding hills – screams, the claxon
of the bumpers, the Killers' sublime key-

change bigging up the thrills in brittle
air: behind you, there, then here, then
girls and music, deciduously, everywhere.

Connection

Gas. Before excavating, telephone Wrexham 53181.

There's no-one at the end
of that line now. Codes
mature, numbers clinch

in new concatenations.

Tap into disconnection;
speak in the teeth of the dud
hum; clear the job with the dead

foreman and dig for lines
like arteries from here
to somewhere, yesterday.

Wine Labels

for Patrick Crotty

1. Colli di Castelfranci (Greco di Tufo)

Medieval lunar:
fat winemoon over
sectored hills and
pale city,
pointillist grapes
like hundreds and thousands.

2. Andrew Will (Merlot)

Would suit a pack
of cigarettes: white box
and black with nineteen–
twenties lines.
       Uncork, light
up, inhale the beef
of Washington State.

3. Coste e Fossati (Dolcetto)

Brede of pitched roofs –
hipped and half-hipped
with catslides and sweet
dormers; white slashes
of gable-end
       intimating thoroughfares.

4. Personalised Wedding Label (Champagne)

Nick and Lara in a bubbly
clinch, fronting their own
bottle. Forever
demi-sec.

5. Mulderbosch (Sauvignon Blanc)

Ribbon and wax
sealing a treaty,
running from cap to convex
hill of glass,

made to be broken.

Tomb Graffiti

On the helmet, a W cut
as two Vs in a clinch;

on the gorget, T and ALJ;
on the tiny oval window

of a face, like scars, IB, JH;
nothing on the epaulière;

on the stumps of praying
arms, FR 4 PS, TRU LUV,

a solitary K; on the elbow
couters, TR, BS; on the corslet,

small as a child's, IB (again),
EC, BN, a little r; on the skirt

of tasses, PPP, a perfect O;
on the greaves and bullnose

sabatons, N, AA, TT (together,
by one hand) –

              this alabaster spell.

Mummies

1. Three bodies, Montefalco

My desiccated dears.
In Wales we'd water
you. Here, they keep
you like birds in air-
tight cases, your eyes
tapping the glass
for crumbs of coins.

2. Saint Zita, Lucca

Dressed for a wedding.
Your hands are turnip-roots
forever guarding the soil
of your private parts.

3. St John Vianney, Ars

Curé –

preserve us
from dryness;
give us
air and space;

close our eyes
to the Nikon flashes
shooting back
from your gilt cage.

5. Saint Bernadette Soubirous, Nevers

Greta Garbo
of the incorruptibles,
your silent film paused
in expectation
       of the blessed talkies.

September Song

From the Welsh of Waldo Williams.

The tree of worlds shoots
higher and September
is the space;

the sunstar, ripe and pun–
gent, bows down its
seasoned face.

Under its store of summer
the prime branch
ramifies

through loaded stillness into
our own hearts'
open skies.

And in this border season,
another light
on harm –

at the hub of endless murder
September's sub–
song's calm.

Acknowledgements

Thanks are due to the editors of the following publications, in which some of the poems in this volume first appeared: *Agenda*, Carcanet's *Oxford Poets 2007: An Anthology*, *Modern Poetry in Translation*, *New Welsh Review*, *Planet: The Welsh Internationalist*, *PN Review*, *poems.com*, *Poetry Wales*, *Scintilla*, *The Wolf.*

Part of the 'Aerial' sequence was broadcast on the BBC Radio Wales Arts Show.

In the 'Ideal City' sequence, there are similarities between the (imagined) architect, Etienne de Barras, and the French architect Claude-Nicolas Ledoux (1736–1806). Some of the details in 'Architect' are taken from the entry on Hailey in the Pevsner *Architectural Guide to Oxfordshire* (1974).

The 'Aerial' sequence is the result of a collaborative venture with the Royal Commission on the Ancient and Historical Monuments of Wales/Comisiwn Brenhinol Henebion Cymru – a reconnaissance flight in a Cessna 172 over Pembrokeshire in bright light on 23 October 2007. I am grateful to Toby Driver, Aerial Survey Project Manager at RCAHMW, to the pilot, Martin Nichols, and to the Sir David Hughes Parry fund at Aberystwyth University for making this project possible.